The Ultimatıide
for Cancer　　　　, ıheir
Family and Friends

Zoe Hellman Bsc SRD

Emerald Guides
www.emeraldpublishing.co.uk

ISBN 9781847160843

Printed by Biddles Ltd Kings Lynn Norfolk

Cover design by Donna McCann

Whilst every effort has been made to ensure that the information
contained within this book is correct at the time of going to
press, the author and publisher can take no responsibility for
the errors or omissions contained within.

Contents

Introduction

Whilst working in the NHS, I frequently met people diagnosed with cancer who had adopted 'alternative' nutritional advice from various unreliable sources. The advice was trusted as it was presented in such a way that suggested the dietary principles were safe and well researched.

These 'alternative' diets are often strict, eliminating essential food groups, and hence nutrients from the diet. Unfortunately some of the people I met had, unknowingly, severely compromised their nutritional status and as a consequence were unable to tolerate effective levels of cancer treatment or were unable to do simple everyday tasks due a lack of energy and strength.

This was my motivation; to write a book that keeps it simple – no gimmicks – just reliable information and advice.

Around 80% of people diagnosed with cancer experience some degree of under-nutrition. Diet and health are inextricably linked and the awareness of just how important nutrition is for those with cancer is growing. Nutritional therapy is now understood to be an essential part of cancer treatment, rather than simply as an adjunct or an afterthought.

This book provides comprehensive information on nutritional therapy for those affected by cancer, based on the latest research and clinical practice, showing *why* and *how* to apply important principles to the diet.

There are over 200 different types of cancer, each one bringing different nutritional difficulties. This book has been developed to provide information and advice to anyone affected by any type cancer, tackling the most common nutritional issues in a simple and practical way.

Following each chapter there is space to make notes. This space could be used in a number of different ways; to jot down questions to ask during a consultation with a health professional, to document a 'to do' list or action plan or simply to make notes of any thoughts relevant to the chapter.

A few terms explained

Nutritional status:	This term refers to the state of the body related to the consumption and utilisation of nutrition.
Under-nutrition:	This term refers to a state in which the consumption and utilisation of nutrition is insufficient to meet the needs of the body.

Nutritional Therapy: This is a term used to describe the application of scientific understanding into practical dietary principles to maintain and promote health and treat disease.

Chapter One

How Cancer Affects Nutritional Status

Not everyone who is diagnosed with cancer experiences nutritional problems. However, many people experience nutritional problems before they are diagnosed with cancer- losing weight and suffering symptoms such as nausea – and may become depleted in nutrients early on. In addition, some cancer treatments are known to have negative effects on nutritional status – so for those people not experiencing nutritional problems early on, it would be sensible to consider adopting nutrition therapy principles to help 'build up' for treatment.

Regardless of current nutritional status, it is important to engage in some form of nutritional therapy as early as possible, as up to 80% of people diagnosed with cancer experience some degree of under-nutrition at some point during cancer treatment.

Cancer can have an impact on nutritional status in a number of different ways.

Weight loss is a common symptom experienced by people with cancer. Around 4 out of 10 people (40%) have unintentional weight loss when their cancer is diagnosed. The commonly used terms; cachexia (kak ex ee a) or wasting syndrome describe the complex state of weight loss and under-nutrition associated with cancer. Cachexia comes from the Greek words Kakos, meaning 'bad' and Hexis, meaning 'condition'.

The weight loss caused by cancer is associated with losses of both muscle and fat. It is caused by a combination of changes in metabolism and often a reduction in dietary intake, due to the side effects of the cancer and its treatment. The weight loss caused by cancer is very different to weight loss through diet or exercise where the majority of weight loss is fat.

Changes in metabolism impacting on nutritional status

The bodies' normal process of metabolism (the breakdown and usage of the different nutrients) is affected by cancer. Cancer actually changes the way our body breaks down and uses fat, protein and carbohydrates.

Changes in metabolism caused by cancer:

- Changes in fat metabolism – The stores of fat in the body are broken down much more quickly and the rate that the body stores fat is reduced. This means that overall stores of body fat are decreased.

- Changes in protein metabolism – The human body does not have any stores or reserves of protein. This is because all the protein within the body has important functions to fulfil. Most of the protein within the body is used to make up muscle, but protein also plays a major role in the immune system. Cancer causes the breakdown of these vital body proteins and reduces the generation of new proteins. When the body breaks down its own proteins, a process known as catabolism, this can have effects on body weight, muscle strength, organ function and the immune system.
- Changes in carbohydrate metabolism – The body is not able to use carbohydrate as efficiently as should. This inefficiency may account for up to 300kcals a day of lost energy.

Due to these changes in metabolism, it can be very difficult to reverse weight loss associated with cancer and this is why early and continued nutritional therapy is really important. Trying to *protect and minimise* the loss of body proteins and fat stores should be a major goal of nutritional therapy.

In addition to these changes in metabolism, cancer also increases Basic Metabolic Rate (BMR). BMR is the rate at which food (calories) is used up. When BMR is raised, the body is said to be in a state called 'hyper metabolism'. This means that the bodies' overall nutritional requirements are increased. So, despite eating a seemingly sufficient diet, weight may be lost because the body is burning calories much faster than normal.

Figure 1.1 Hierarchy of metabolism

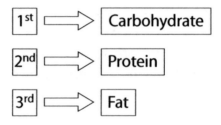

Figure 1.1 illustrates the hierarchy of metabolism – the way that different food groups are used as energy in the body. Figure 1.1 shows that the first source of energy the body will use is carbohydrates. During periods of reduced dietary intake or more specifically reduced carbohydrate intake, body proteins and then fat stores are called upon for energy to fuel the body. In a state of hyper metabolism, these energy sources are called upon more quickly to ensure there is sufficient fuel for the body.

If the way different food groups are used for energy is considered, it is clear that in the first instance, having sufficient carbohydrates is crucial to help protect against the breakdown of body proteins and fat stores.

Loss of appetite impacting on nutritional status

Loss of appetite may sometimes be called anorexia. It is a common symptom of cancer. Appetite is created by, and controlled through, complex processes in the body. The environment around us and how we think and feel can also influence appetite. The loss of appetite often experienced by people with cancer is thought to be caused, in part, by the cancer itself. It is thought that cancer releases chemicals into the body, which directly decrease appetite. Loss of appetite may also be experienced due to symptoms of the cancer and side effects of treatment.

Whatever the cause, loss of appetite has major effects for people with cancer and can be difficult to overcome. It is important to try and identify the causes for the loss of appetite, in order to use specific nutritional therapy to help overcome them.

Symptoms of cancer impacting on nutritional status

As already discussed, weight loss, due to a combination of loss of appetite and changes in metabolism, is a major symptom of cancer. Tiredness and fatigue are also common side-effects with most types of cancers. There are also other less obvious, or less well-known symptoms, which can become major obstacles to optimising nutritional intake for people with cancer.

Different types of cancer can have specific nutritional problems associated with them and each need to be identified and individually addressed.

The diagnosis of cancer impacting on nutritional status

Coping with a diagnosis of cancer may have an affect on eating and drinking. A diagnosis of cancer can be life changing and it can be frightening. It may cause feelings of anxiety, low mood and around 40% of people with cancer report difficulties concentrating and a lack of energy. Support during this difficult time is essential for everyone and counselling may help to cope.

Cancer treatment impacting on nutritional status

Cancer treatments may have side effects which can contribute to under-nutrition. Some treatments may have a direct impact on a person's ability to eat and in some cases nutritional support may be required.

A note on weight gain

Some cancer treatments can in fact contribute to weight gain. However, the weight gain experienced by some may be associated with the natural aging process, rather than the treatment itself.

Being a healthy weight is important for health, but actively trying to lose weight whilst undergoing cancer treatment is certainly not advisable. During treatment, having a healthy, well-balanced diet may help to prevent gains in weight. Once treatment is complete, it may be useful to seek support from a registered dietitian, support group or slimming club.

The most effective way to lose weight is by focusing on having a healthy, balanced diet and increasing physical activity levels.

Key Points

Cancer can have an impact on nutritional status in a number of different ways. Each problem requires specific nutritional therapy to address and help overcome it.

Readers Notes on Chapter One: How Cancer affects Nutritional Status.

Chapter Two

Why Nutrition is so Important for People with Cancer

The physical effects of under-nutrition, namely weight loss, are easy to recognise. However, under-nutrition can affect all body cells, organs and functions and can also have an impact on social and psychological health.

Being well nourished can help a person to:

- Cope with the side effects of cancer treatment.
- Handle the most beneficial dose of certain cancer treatments.
- Recover and heal.
- Fight off infections.
- Feel strong.
- Maintain energy levels.
- Have a shorter hospital stay.

> **When the body is under-nourished all body functions can be affected.**

An inadequate intake of nutrients, not only means an inadequate intake of energy, but also means a lack of essential vitamins and minerals. And hence, the effects of under-nutrition can be wide ranging.

The effect of under-nutrition on body functions

The body is made up of billions of body cells that maintain life and growth. Body cells are produced, perform a function and then die. Some body cells tend to live, performing their function, for longer than others.

Body cells that only live for a short period of time (i.e. are produced, perform a function and then die relatively quickly), are known as 'rapid turnover' cells. These cells can be seriously affected by under-nutrition because constant supplies of nutrients are needed to produce them. Therefore the functions of the body that uses these rapid turnover cells can also be seriously affected by under-nutrition.

Functions of the body, which use rapid turnover cells include:

1. Digestion
2. Blood cell production
3. Immunity
4. Healing

1. Digestion

The lining of the digestive system, called the epithelium, absorbs nutrients from food and protects the body from infection. The epithelium acts as a gateway, letting nutrients in and working to keep infections out.

In order to develop an infection, from bacteria or viruses, they must first gain access to the body. This could be, for example, through cuts or grazes, or though the digestive system. So if the epithelium (the body's gateway) is not working efficiently, the body can become at risk of infection.

If the cells that make up the epithelium are not supplied with sufficient nutrients, the epithelium can become weak and inefficient: The bodies' ability to effectively absorb the nutrients from food is reduced and the risk of becoming under- nourished is increased.

2. Blood cell production

Under-nutrition can reduce the production of blood cells. Having a lack of red blood cells (called anaemia), reduces the bodies' capability to carry oxygen from the lungs and around the body, which can lead to tiredness and shortness of breath. Without a constant fresh supply of oxygen, body cells become unable to function, so all body functions can be affected.

3. Immunity

The body cells that work to protect the body from infection can be significantly affected by under-nutrition, which can lead to an increased risk of infections.

The immune system protects the body from infection in two different ways:

A. Protection against infections entering the body (protection and defence immunity)
B. Protection from infections which have already entered the body (immune cell immunity)

The skin and the lining of the digestive system provide protection and defence immunity. Under-nutrition reduces this type of immunity by affecting these defence systems. A lack of nutrients can cause skin to become weaker, breaking more easily, and failing to protect infections from entering the body. The lining of the digestive system (the epithelium) becomes weak without a constant supply of nutrients, increasing the likelihood of infections entering the body.

Under-nutrition directly affects the cells of the immune system, leading to a reduction in their number and strength. The loss of body proteins, caused by cancer associated weight loss, also has an impact on immune cells, as body proteins are used to produce them.

4. Healing

The bodies' ability to heal itself can be affected by under-nutrition. Wounds find it difficult to heal, as the extra nutrients needed to rebuild body cells are in short supply.

> **Scientific evidence shows that people who are well nourished are able to heal and recover faster than those who are under nourished.**

The effect of muscle loss on body functions

Cancer causes the loss of fat stores and body proteins. The majority of body proteins are muscles. It is commonly believed that when muscle is lost it is from the muscles used for mobility and strength such the arms and legs. However, when muscle is lost, it can be lost from any muscle within the body, including those in the heart and lungs.

The main role of the lungs is to inhale air to gather oxygen for the blood. The main role of the heart is to pump blood around every part of the body. When muscle from the heart and lungs is lost these essential processes can be affected.

An under-nourished heart:

- Has reduced strength to pump blood around the body.
- Pumps smaller amounts of blood at one time.

Under-nourished lungs:

- Have a reduced ability to inhale air.
- Have a reduced amount of air that can be inhaled.
- Have a reduced overall ability to get oxygen into the blood.

The effect of under-nutrition on cancer treatment

Good nutrition is so important for people with cancer because there is a direct link between nutritional status and cancer treatment. It is well known that the success of cancer treatments is influenced by a person's ability to tolerate it, which in-turn may be affected by their nutritional status.

In the first instance, the decision to undertake a cancer treatment takes into consideration a persons' nutritional status. Those who are better nourished are able to handle certain cancer treatments better.

In addition, the strength of some cancer treatments will also take a persons' nutritional status into account. Some cancer treatments are exhausting and place great demands on the body. Those who are significantly under-nourished may need to be given weaker treatment and those who are under-weight may need to be given lower doses.

Other impacts of under-nutrition on cancer treatment include:

- An increased risk of experiencing side-effects.
- Potentially reduced beneficial responses.
- Increased complication rates and recovery time.

It is important to remember that working to maintain nutritional status is not only essential to help maintain energy levels and health, but is crucial for the optimum response to, and recovery from, cancer treatment.

The social and psychological effects of under-nutrition

Under-nutrition can have effects on social and psychological health. Being under-nourished is associated with:

- A reduced ability to concentrate.
- A lack of initiative.
- Feelings of apathy and low mood.
- Irritability.

Weight loss and a loss of appetite are often major concerns to a person with cancer and their loved ones around them. Weight loss and associated changes in appearance can affect a person's self-image and confidence, and can be a constant daily reminder of illness. A loss of appetite can have a negative impact of the quality of a person's social life, as often eating and drinking plays a part. And a lack of energy can affect the ability to carry out daily activities, like shopping and cleaning which may have an impact on independence.

In addition to engaging with nutritional therapy, sometimes simply being aware of how under-nutrition can affect social and psychological spheres, and acknowledging them as an aspect of the cancer and its treatment, rather than being anything intentional, can help to deal with them.

Key points

A good nutritional status can help:

✓ To be able to handle cancer treatment
✓ To possibly handle higher doses of cancer treatment
✓ The body to recover and heal
✓ The body to be stronger, with more energy to undertake activities of everyday life
✓ To maintain independence
✓ To be more confident
✓ To be able to ward off feelings of apathy and low mood
✓ To promote a robust immune system
✓ To maintain concentration levels

Readers Notes on Chapter Two: Why Nutrition is so Important for People with Cancer.

Chapter Three

Understanding and Support

Providing nourishment is often naturally felt to be a way of showing care and affection: The 'food as love syndrome'. As loved ones often want to show affection for someone when they are unwell, food can sometimes become a contentious issue. Someone who has lost their appetite or feels too unwell to eat may feel under pressure to avoid disappointing those who have made the effort to prepare a meal for them. Meal times can cause worry and friction, taking the pleasure out of eating all together.

The key to easing friction over food is to not associate food with personal feelings and to try and share an understanding. Talking about issues surrounding eating is vital. It may be easier to talk about these issues during a consultation with a registered dietitian or a support worker.

Eating is not just an adjunct to life, such as taking medicines or undergoing treatment, but is an integral part of everyday life. Eating habits evolve over a lifetime and often become deeply ingrained. Having to change these habits can often be really difficult and have a big impact on life, just like changing any other habit that has become deeply ingrained, such as giving up smoking. Acknowledging that making changes to eating can, in itself, cause anxiety could help to start easing tensions.

Food shopping, preparation, and mealtimes may need to change completely from the 'norm', so planning ahead is important. Learning about and being aware of how dietary intake is affected, for example by a reduced appetite, loss of smell, changes in taste or tiredness can really help to 'set the scene' for how food can fit it more comfortably.

Some people affected by cancer may have difficulties in shopping and preparing meals so may need some additional support or assistance during this time. It may be useful to get a referral to an occupational therapist for advice on relevant local support networks and equipment available or modifications around the house that can help make life a little easier.

There are different local support networks that could offer help with shopping for and preparing food. Adaptations to everyday equipment in the kitchen can help make preparing food much easier. For example there is equipment to open bottles and cans easily, swivel taps, easy grip or easy use cutlery, easy to use scissors, trolleys and a various designs of plates, dishes and trays that can all make preparing food and eating much easier.

Readers Notes on Chapter Three: Understanding and Support.

Chapter Four

How to Measure Nutritional Status

There are a number of ways to measure nutritional status which look at different aspects of the body like dimensions, composition and function. Some measurements can be easily done at home, whilst others need to be done together with a health professional. A set of monitoring forms can be found in the appendices to make documenting and tracking nutritional status as easy as possible.

Measuring and monitoring nutritional status can provide important details to inform and guide nutritional therapy and cancer treatment. For those who need it, a registered dietitian should undertake individual full nutritional assessments and ongoing monitoring alongside cancer treatment.

Measuring nutritional status at home

In order to measure and monitor nutritional status at home, a few simple assessments can be done. Both objective and subjective assessment can be useful.

Objective measurements of nutritional status

Body Mass Index

Body Mass Index (BMI) is based on a person's height and weight. It is used to provide a broad indicator of nutritional status. BMI only looks at weight and height – it is unable to actually distinguish body composition, i.e. what proportions of the body are fat, or muscle, so may not be an accurate representation of nutritional status in people who have suffered muscle loss.

$$BMI = \frac{Weight\ (kg)}{Height2\ (m)}$$

BMI <17 = **Seriously underweight**
BMI 17–20 = **Underweight**
BMI 20–25 = **Healthy weight**
BMI 26–30 = **Overweight**
BMI >30 = **Very overweight**

For example if a person is 50kg and 1.7m:

$$BMI = \frac{50kg}{2.89} = 17.3\ kg/m^2 = Underweight$$

Percentage weight loss

A useful indication of nutritional status is not looking simply at the *amount* of weight that has been has lost, but the percentage of total body weight lost over a certain period. This can give a more accurate picture of what is going on.

% Weight Loss =

$$\frac{\text{Usual weight (kg)} - \text{Current Weight (kg)}}{\text{Usual Weight (kg)}} \times 100$$

For example if a person's usual weight is 60kg and 6 months later is 50kg:

$$\% \text{ Weight Loss} = \frac{60 - 50}{60} \times 100 = 16.6\%$$

In reality, small amounts of weight loss can be easy to miss. A 5% weight loss in a 50kg person is only a loss of just 2.5kg. Monitoring of weight and other measurements of nutritional status helps to ensure changes are picked up quickly.

If weight loss is less than 5% = This is not considered a significant amount of weight loss unless it is likely to be ongoing. However, for those people with cancer, weight loss is likely to be ongoing. This would therefore indicate that nutritional therapy should be engaged with.

If weight loss is 10–20% = This is considered a significant amount of weight loss. Working together with a registered dietitian, nutritional therapy should certainly be engaged with or increased.

If weight loss is greater than 20% = This is considered severe weight loss. Working together with a registered dietitian, nutritional therapy should certainly be engaged with or increased.

Subjective measurements of nutritional status

Subjective measurements are just as important in the assessment of nutritional status as objective measurements. Subjective measurements can help to identify and understand specific nutritional problems and help to provide direction for appropriate nutritional therapy. If objective measurements, such as weight are unattainable the following questions can help to provide information on nutritional status.

- Have you unintentionally lost weight?
- Do you feel that your clothes are looser?
- How long have your clothes felt loose for?
- Have you had to adjust the tightness of your belt or watch strap recently? If so, how many notches have you adjusted by?
- Do you feel that you have experienced muscle wasting?
- Do you feel that you have experienced a reduction in fat stores?
- Are you currently retaining fluid? If so, where?

It can be useful to regularly document answers to the following questions, to help monitor changes in nutritional status.

Eating patterns

- Have you been experiencing any changes in your usual dietary intake? If so, how long have been experiencing them?
- What percentage of your usual dietary intake are you managing to eat at the moment?
- Has the consistency of your diet needed to be changed? If so, how has this changed and is the need continuous or intermittent?
- Do you have any persistent symptoms that are affecting your food intake? Outline these symptoms and how they affect your intake.

Bowel habits

- Are you suffering from diahorrea? If so, is it continuous or intermittent?
- Are you suffering from constipation? If so, is it continuous or intermittent?

Activity

- Has your ability to carry out activities of everyday life changed? If so, how?
- Has your ability to provide and prepare food changed? If so, how?

Measuring nutritional status with a health professional

Nutritional status screening

Every health centre should have a nutritional status screening tool, which is undertaken at a first outpatient appointment and on every hospital admission. A number of nutrition screening tools are used within health centres that take into consideration factors such as; diagnosis, weight changes, appetite changes and ability to eat. It can be useful to become familiar with the local nutrition screening tool and ensure that it has been completed accurately and followed up appropriately.

Bioelectrical Impedance Analysis (BIA)

Bioelectrical impedance analysis (BIA) uses a machine, which can determine the composition of the body.

Figure 1.2 Body composition

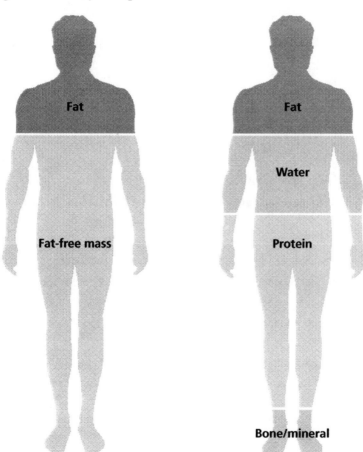

A single BIA measurement can show current body composition, which health professionals can compare with 'ideal' compositions. If sequential BIA measurements are taken, changes in a person's body composition over a period of time can be tracked – which can be very useful.

Measurements to assess changes in body composition

1. **Fat stores**

   Tricep Skin Fold Thickness (TSF)

2. **Levels of body proteins**

   Grip strength
   Mid arm Muscle Circumference (MAMC)

As cancer can lead to changes in body composition, i.e. body proteins and fat stores are often lost, it is beneficial to have measurements to assess changes in body composition undertaken regularly, to help provide accurate monitoring of nutritional status and guide appropriate and sufficient nutritional therapy. To interpret the measurements for each of these techniques, there are standard reference range charts that a health professional will use.

Tricep Skin Fold Thickness (TSF)

A skin fold calliper is used to measure the thickness of the tricep area to indicate body fat stores.

Grip strength

Grip strength is a functional measurement of nutritional status. A device called a handgrip dynamometer is used to test the strength of the non-dominant hand's grip. This indicates levels of muscle strength and hence levels of body proteins.

Functional strength is known to improve much more quickly following improvements in nutritional status compared with any other measurement of nutritional status, providing a really useful early sign of improvement. This can sometimes be a great motivator; to see the response from the body to efforts of nutritional therapy.

Mid Arm Muscle Circumference (MAMC)

Measurements of the circumference of the non-dominant arm, together with measurements of TSF provide an indication of muscle mass and hence levels of body proteins.

Biochemical tests of nutritional status

Using biochemical tests (from urine or blood samples) alone to determine nutritional status are not very reliable or useful.

Many non-nutritional factors may influence biochemical results, making their accuracy low. Cancer and cancer treatments may also affect results. However, biochemical tests can be useful, when used together with other measurements, to provide a broad picture of nutritional status and changes over a period of time.

Blood tests for proteins

Certain proteins can be found in the blood stream and can give some information on nutritional status, as under-nutrition causes levels of these proteins to drop. However, these are not very reliable as there are other non-nutritional factors which can also make these protein levels to drop such as; stress, fluid balances within the body and administration of blood products.

Blood tests for vitamin and minerals

A number of biochemical tests can be carried out to determine vitamin and mineral levels in the blood and urine. Together with examination of physical symptoms and an accurate dietary history analysis, risk of deficiency can be assessed and treated accordingly.

The presence of symptoms, such as diahorrea may indicate dietary absorption problems and losses of certain vitamins and minerals. Some medications can also affect the absorption of certain vitamins and minerals from food but the prescribing health professional should review the need for deficiency testing and supplementation.

Nitrogen balance

When protein is broken down and used, it is broken down into amino acids. One of the major components of amino acids is nitrogen. If there is sufficient protein in the diet the body will use what it needs and then get rid of what it doesn't in the urine and usefully, nitrogen levels can be then be detected. Measuring nitrogen balance (nitrogen in – nitrogen out) is one way of learning how the body is breaking down and using proteins from the diet and the body.

Nitrogen balance can be a useful indicator of whether any benefit has been achieved in response to nutritional therapy. In order to measure nitrogen balance, dietary protein intake is monitored and urine is collected over a 24 hours period, which can then be analysed.

If more nitrogen is found to be in the urine than is eaten, this is known as a 'positive nitrogen balance'. This shows that there is more nitrogen around, hence protein, than the body actually needs, indicating that enough protein is being eaten to cover current protein requirements.

If less nitrogen is found to be in the urine than is eaten, this is known as a 'negative nitrogen balance'. The body needs more nitrogen, hence protein, than it is actually getting, showing that levels of body proteins are probably being broken down to provide the deficit – therefore nutritional status is likely to be affected. Some people with cancer may suffer from a 'negative nitrogen balance' despite consuming sufficient protein, due to metabolic changes associated with cancer.

Readers Notes on Chapter Four: How to Measure Nutritional Status.

Chapter Five

The Goals of Nutrition Therapy

Having clear, well-defined goals increases the likelihood that people will reach them. Before engaging with nutritional therapy, clear goals need to be set, not only to guide the therapy itself, but to measure its effects. The goals of nutritional therapy will be different for everyone and may change over time.

Optimal nutritional status would seem like the ultimate goal for everyone. However, optimal nutritional status may not be a suitable goal for those with cancer. The changes in metabolism caused by cancer and the side effects of cancer mean that, despite an increase in dietary intake, weight gain is often difficult to achieve.

Therefore, nutritional therapy should aim to *maintain and preserve* weight, rather than replace weight that may already have been lost. Maintaining weight during cancer treatment is an important goal and a great success if achieved.

A waiver from certain religious dietary restrictions is often granted for cancer sufferers undergoing treatment. For people of certain religions, it may advisable to consider the importance of maintaining nutritional status and consult religious leaders.

> **It is important that goals are realistic and achievable.**

The goals of nutritional therapy during cancer treatment will be different for everyone. They may be to:

- Prevent or reverse certain nutrient deficiencies.
- Preserve body proteins.
- Ease symptoms of cancer.
- Improve tolerance to cancer treatment.
- Minimise side effects of cancer treatment.
- Maintain energy and strength for everyday life.
- Protect immune functions.
- Aid wound healing and recovery.
- Maintain independence.
- Improve well-being.

When discussing and setting goals, focus on what is important and what is achievable.

Setting some simple measurable goals can help to monitor progress. For example:

- To be able to go for a walk.
- To be able to maintain current weight and/or body composition.
- To increase strength to recover quicker from treatment days.

- To avoid catching an infection.
- To be able to sit down to a meal without feeling nauseous.
- To be able to enjoy meal times.
- To have the energy to go to the shops.

Writing out goals and displaying them somewhere they can easily be seen can be a good motivator. And regularly reviewing goals, helps to ensure they are relevant and achievable.

Food diaries

Before embarking on well-planned nutritional therapy, keeping a food diary may be useful. Keeping food diaries can show aspects of eating habits, which may not have been apparent otherwise. They provide an insight into eating habits and can prove to be a helpful monitoring tool as treatment is progressed through. It is not a good idea to keep a constant food diary, as this can be a daunting task and may not actually be helpful. But, keeping a diary for a few days prior to initiating nutritional therapy and regularly throughout treatment can be useful. Food diaries can help to build an idea of patterns that are positive to eating and also those which are not so positive to eating and can be used to mould nutritional therapy for success.

Food diaries do not necessarily have to simply be a record of everything that has been eaten. Some people may find it useful to record details that are relevant to their goals. For example, if the goal is to aim to reduce nausea at mealtimes, then keeping a record that focuses on the issues surrounding nausea could be useful (what lead up to the feelings of nausea, what was able to be eaten at the mealtime, was there anything that helped to ease the nausea etc).

After keeping a food diary, it is important to spend time looking over the information, looking for patterns to help guide nutritional therapy. Some people find it useful to do this during a consultation with a registered dietitian or health professional.

Example of a food diary: write down the answer to the following questions when you eat.

When?

Where?

What?

Why?

How Much?

Did you have any symptoms affecting dietary intake? If yes, did anything help to ease them?

Readers Notes on Chapter Five: The Goals of Nutrition Therapy.

Chapter Six

Nutritional Therapy

Nutritional Therapy is a term used to describe the application of scientific understanding into practical dietary principles to maintain and promote health and treat disease.

There are a range of levels of nutritional therapy, to help maintain and promote health and treat cancer associated problems. The key levels of nutritional therapy are:

1. As far as possible, ensure a well balanced diet
2. Observe basic food hygiene principles to reduce the risk of infection
3. Identify problems affecting nutritional intake and use dietary and practical techniques to help overcome them
4. If required, increase the nutritional content of the diet by fortification
5. If required, increase the nutritional content of the diet by using nutritional supplements
6. If required, increase the nutritional content of the diet by using artificial nutrition support

The level of nutritional therapy that is needed will be different for everyone and may fluctuate over the course of treatment. Some of the techniques discussed within this chapter may not be appropriate for everyone. **Always** consult a registered dietitian or health professional before engaging with any kind of nutritional therapy and again if the problems persists.

Top Tips for Nutritional Therapy

✓ Introduce a few small changes at a time, as this allows the body and mind to adapt, increasing the likelihood of the changes being stuck to.
✓ Try out lots different things to find the solution that works best.
✓ Make time for considering and working on nutritional status, as it is so important.
✓ Plan, Plan, Plan – In order to engage with nutrition therapy, planning and preparation needs to be done.
✓ Regularly review progress – In order to ensure that relevant goals are being focused on.

A well balanced diet

It is well known that nutrition has a direct impact on health. There are many different 'alternative' diets that are promoted for people suffering from cancer, the claims of which can sometimes be confusing. Some 'alternative' diets are presented in a way which suggests they are safe and well researched, so the advice is often trusted. Many of these types of diets are restrictive, eliminating essential food groups and nutrients, which can severely compromise a person's nutritional status, therefore having a direct and *significant* negative impact on health.

Some diets may claim to 'cure cancer' or 'shrink a tumour', but there is no reliable scientific evidence to support these claims.

There is however, a wealth of reliable scientific evidence which shows that a healthy, balanced diet supports the human body for good health and well being: A healthy, balanced diet is vital for good health and there is no exception for people with cancer.

There is also a wealth of reliable scientific evidence which shows that people who are well nourished are able to; cope with the side effects of cancer treatment better, handle the most beneficial dose of certain cancer treatments, recover and heal faster and have shorter hospital stays.

No one single food or food group can provide the human body with all the nutrients it needs, so having a varied diet is key. However, the body does requires different nutrients in differing amounts, so it stands to reason that different food groups are needed in differing proportions.

For good health the body needs: Regular meals which are based on fibre-rich starchy carbohydrates (like pasta, bread, rice, potatoes or cereals), with plenty of fruit and vegetables (at least five portions every day), some lean or low-fat protein-rich foods (such as meat, fish, eggs, lentils, milk and dairy) and a small amount of healthy fats. Not forgetting plenty of fluids (6–8 glasses or around 1.2 litres a day) to keep the body hydrated.

Focus on carbohydrates

There are two types of carbohydrate; sugars and starch. The majority of the energy in the diet should come from fibre-rich starchy carbohydrates like brown bread, cereals, rice, pasta and potatoes. Sugary carbohydrates, like those found in honey, chocolate, cakes, biscuits and fizzy drinks, can also provide an important source of energy, particularly if someone has a poor appetite or reduced ability to eat. If someone has a poor appetite or reduced ability to eat, then aiming for a fibre-rich diet may not be appropriate, as it tends to fill up the stomach without many calories or other nutrients.

Carbohydrates could help to preserve body proteins.

All body cells need a constant supply of fuel. Glucose is the main source of fuel for the body. When carbohydrates are eaten, the body breaks them down into their simplest form – glucose. But, if carbohydrates are in short supply, glucose can also be obtained by breaking down body proteins. If there are insufficient supplies of carbohydrates for body fuel, body proteins are raided. In order to help to preserve body proteins, an adequate amount of carbohydrates is vital. But as cancer causes changes in carbohydrate metabolism (by reducing its efficiency), the amount of carbohydrate needed to help preserve body proteins is increased. Sugary carbohydrates found in sugary drinks, chocolate and sweets could be an excellent way to provide energy for the body when someone has a poor appetite.

Focus on fruit and vegetables

A healthy diet consists of at least five portions of fruit and vegetables every day, these can be fresh, frozen, dried or tinned. Roughly, a portion of fruit and vegetables fits within the palm of the hand.

Focus on protein

Proteins are made up from smaller parts called amino acids. There are 20 different types of amino acids. It is these small amino acids, often called the building blocks of life that the body uses to build and repair itself. Body processes need all of the 20 different amino acids to work properly.

Amino acids are found in two groups:

1. Non-essential amino acids – these types of amino acids can be made within the body from the ingredients of other amino acids. There are 12 different types of non-essential amino acids.
2. Essential amino acids – these types of amino acids cannot be made within the body. The only way that the body can get some is from the diet. There are 8 different types of essential amino acids.

Different protein rich foods contain different amounts and combinations of amino acids. This is why the choice of protein rich foods is important, as it can have an impact on whether there are sufficient amino acids in the diet to make sure that the body is able to work properly.

The biological value of different protein rich foods is the measure of how sufficient it is in all the amino acids needed for the body. Foods classed as high biological value are those that are really good sources of all the essential amino acids needed for the body. Foods classed as low biological value are those that do not have all the essential amino acids needed for the body.

> **For those people with increased nutritional requirements or those with reduced dietary intakes, choosing protein sources that are high biological value can help to prevent under-nutrition.**

High biological value protein sources include; protein from animal sources, such as meat and dairy products, fish, eggs, beans, lentils and soya products. Low biological value protein sources include; bread, vegetables, nuts, and seeds.

Focus on healthy fats

Although a high fat diet is unhealthy, a healthy diet does include some 'healthy' fats.

Saturated fat – This type of fat is unhealthy as it can increase the amount of cholesterol in the blood which increases the risks of developing high blood pressure, stroke and heart disease. Saturated fats are found in; cakes, biscuits, crisps, pastry, butter and lard, cream, cheese.

Unsaturated fat – This type of fat does not tend to increase the amount of cholesterol in the blood. Unsaturated fats also provide some vitamins and essential fatty acids – an important part of a healthy diet. Unsaturated fats are found in; oily fish, avocados, nuts and seeds, sunflower, rapeseed and olive oil spreads and vegetable oils.

Focus on vitamin and minerals

A healthy, balanced diet should provide all the vitamins and minerals the body needs. However, increased nutritional requirements associated with cancer and decreased dietary intakes, may increase the risk of deficiencies.

Taking vitamin and mineral supplements unsupervised is not advisable, particularly for people with cancer. This is because any deficiencies that are not properly treated could cause a problem. And taking doses of supplements that are not appropriately balanced can lead to imbalances in vitamins and minerals that can be toxic, affect health or interfere with cancer treatment. It is advisable to discuss vitamin and mineral supplementation with a health professional to ensure that any potential deficiencies can be properly identified and safely corrected.

Focus on fluids

The body needs around 6 to 8 glasses (1.2 litres) of fluid, every day. When the weather is warm or the body is active, it will need more.

If someone has a temperature or is losing increased amounts of fluids, through for example vomiting or altered bowel habits, then fluid requirements will increase. Often, people who are unwell may not drink sufficient fluids and this can exacerbate feeling unwell, tiredness and headaches. Ensuring a regular and sufficient fluid intake is vital. Feelings of thirst actually indicate that the body is already getting dehydrated, so drinking before getting thirsty is advisable.

Readers Notes on Chapter Six: Nutritional Therapy – A Well Balanced Diet.

Chapter Seven

Principles of Food Hygiene

Under-nutrition can affect the immune system, increasing the risk of catching an infection. In addition, some cancer treatments may further affect the immune system, which requires specific food safety practices that a registered dietitian or health professional will need to advise on.

It is important for people with cancer to ensure that any potential sources of infection are reduced as much as possible to help prevent infections. One potential source of infection is from food and drink, so following basic food hygiene principles would be sensible.

Food shopping

- Avoid choosing food in damaged or broken packaging.
- Avoid choosing food that is stored in overloaded fridges or freezers as they may not be cooled enough.
- Try to get food shopping home as quickly as possible, and into the fridge or freezer.
- Strictly observe best before or use by dates.

Food storage

- Keep the freezer below −18°C.
- Keep the fridge between 0°C and 5°C.

- Store cooked food at the top of the fridge and raw food at the bottom.
- Any raw meat or fish should be kept at the bottom of the fridge in covered containers.
- Always store eggs in the fridge.
- Never re-freeze thawed food.
- Do not put hot food in the fridge, as this will increase the temperature of all food in the fridge potentially making it unsafe to eat. Cool food at room temperature within an hour after cooking and then chill or freeze.

Food preparation

- Always wash hands before handling any food, in between handling food and doing other things. Dry hands thoroughly as damp hands carry more germs.
- Dry hands using a dedicated hand drying towel or use kitchen paper – do not use a tea towel used for other uses.
- Cover cuts and grazes with a waterproof plaster.
- Keep pets away from the kitchen.
- Disinfect work surfaces regularly.
- Change or wash thoroughly anything used for raw and cooked foods, such as chopping boards, and utensils.
- Wash all fruit and vegetables before eating.
- Wash the top of cans before opening.

Cooking food

- Always thaw frozen food in the fridge, not at room temperature.
- Cook food until it is piping hot all the way through and meat until juices run clear.
- Always observe the cooking instruction on the label.
- Don't let raw meat touch any other foods.
- Do not reheat cooked food.

Eating out

- Ensure food is piping hot when served and cooked all the way through.
- Choose freshly prepared foods from reputable outlets. Avoid salad bars, street vendors, market stalls and ice cream vans.

Readers Notes on Chapter Seven: Principles of Food Hygiene.

Chapter Eight
Problems Affecting Nutritional Intake

Some people with cancer may suffer problems that can interfere with or affect their willingness or ability to eat. Firstly, it is useful to know that there are many different people that can help with problems affecting nutritional intake.

People like family and friends, support workers and specialist cancer nurses can help to manage nutritional problems. Doctors can diagnose specific nutritional problems and advise or prescribe treatment to help overcome them. Pharmacists can help by ensuring that the type and dose of any drug prescribed is safe and they are a source of medication knowledge and expertise. A speech and language therapist can help people with speech problems and swallowing difficulties. They can carry out comprehensive and ongoing swallowing assessments and advise on appropriately safe textures of food and fluids.

Registered dietitians are specifically trained in nutritional therapy and can help deal with nutritional problems. Registered dietitians undertake comprehensive nutritional assessments and monitoring and help to devise and support personalised nutritional therapy plans.

People will experience the symptoms and side effects of cancer and its' treatment differently. In addition, everyone has different food likes and dislikes. Therefore, dietary and practical techniques to overcome any problems will work differently for everyone and it can be a case of 'trial and error' to find what works best.

Dietary and practical techniques to help with the most common nutritional problems associated with cancer are offered in the following section, with examples of implementing them within a sample day's intake.

Remember: Some of the techniques discussed within this chapter may not be appropriate for everyone. **Always** consult a registered dietitian or health professional before engaging with any kind of nutritional therapy and again if the problems persist.

The sample day's intakes help to illustrate suggested dietary techniques. They are not nutritionally balanced menus. Anyone wishing to implement any dietary techniques should consult with a registered dietitian to ensure that their diet is nutritionally balanced whilst meeting their individual needs.

Techniques to help with a small appetite:

- Try to eat 'little and often' having small meals and snacks – Instead of 3 meals a day, try to eat every 2–3 hours or have 6 small meals a day.

- Eat puddings and desserts after a break following main course.
- Friends and family could help by preparing small meals.
- Fortify the diet with additional calories and protein.
- Choose foods that appeal to the senses – for example foods that look really tasty or smell tasty.
- If the smell of food affects appetite, try to have slightly warm or cold foods.
- Have small servings of favorite foods in stock.
- Serve food in small portions – seeing and being expected to eat large portion may further reduce appetite.
- Ensure a stock of easy to make foods are in the cupboards, like soup, boil in the bag or frozen meals.
- Try to avoid drinking half an hour before and during a meal – as this may fill up the stomach with liquids, instead of more nutritious food.
- Sip nutritious drinks throughout the day, like milky or sugary drinks.
- Try a small glass of alcohol half an hour before eating, as this can help to stimulate appetite.
- Try a short walk in the fresh air before eating.
- Make the table or tray look attractive with a table cloth or some flowers.
- Keep nutritious little snacks easy to hand throughout the day.
- Make the most of times when appetite is at its best, often in the mornings.

- Try eating a meal or snack in front of the television or with the radio on in the background – People naturally tend to eat more when there is some form of distraction around them.

Sample menu using techniques to help with a small appetite:

Breakfast	A small bowl of cereal with fortified whole milk and honey
	1 piece of toast with some thickly spread peanut butter and a small banana
	A cup of tea made with some fortified whole milk and 2 sugars
Mid morning	A small milky coffee made from fortified whole milk
	A small pot of full fat fromias frais with a handful of dried fruit sprinkled over the top
Lunch	Take a stroll in the fresh air
	A small tin of creamy soup with a tablespoon of cream mixed in and grated cheese on top and a hard boiled egg

Mid afternoon	A cup of warmed fortified whole milk with 2 chocolate biscuits
Dinner	Have a small glass of favorite wine half an hour before dinner is served
	One small sausage and 1 scoop of mash fortified with cream and grated cheese, and a tablespoon of vegetables with butter melted on the top – garnished with some fresh herbs
	A small bowl of fruit and ice cream
Evening snack	A small slice of cake and a handful of grapes served with a cup of tea made with fortified whole milk and two sugars
Before bed	A small mug of malted drink made with fortified whole milk

Techniques to help with loss of taste or changes in taste:

- Foods that are strong in flavour may be preferred– choose stronger flavours of enjoyed foods like a stronger cheese.

- Sauces, seasoning, gravy, herbs, marinades, pickles and spices can all help to add extra taste to food.
- Experiment with different foods and tastes.
- Avoid very cold or hot foods.
- If meat tastes bitter, try soaking in wine, soya sauce or fruit juices to help minimise this taste.
- If meat tastes bitter, try avoiding foods sweetened with saccharine, as this may exacerbate this taste.
- Clearing the palate with a glass of water with lemon juice in it before eating can help to enhance taste.
- Drink refreshing drinks such as herbal teas, orange juice or lemonade.
- Keep the mouth and teeth clean.
- Rinse or brush teeth before eating.
- Use toothpaste that is non-mint flavour – this may help to reduce aberrant taste in the mouth.
- Try using a spray mister before and during meals.
- If a metallic taste is present; try using plastic or glass utensils.
- If a metallic or bitter taste is present; try sucking on sugar free mints, lemon drops or chewing gum.
- Avoid favorite foods and drinks altogether whilst taste changes persist – as this helps to avoid developing a dislike for them in the long term.
- Avoid the foods that taste strange but re-try every few weeks – as tastes may have changed back to normal. The most common foods affected by changes in taste are; citrus fruits, chocolate, tea and red meats.

To Do:

1. Make a list of all the foods that have been affected by changes in taste.
2. For each food, try to think of the following –
   a. Are there any suitable alternatives that are of similar nutritional content. For example if the taste of red meat is affected, try replacing with poultry, fish, eggs, lentils, pulses or cheeses.
   b. Can the taste be improved by marinating, adding sauces, spices or seasoning?
3. Make a list of anything that is needed to help with changes in taste, for example: non-mint toothpaste, spray mister, glass cutlery.

Techniques to help with diahorrea:

- Avoiding high fibre foods may help – Try low fibre foods such as white bread and rice, pasta and potatoes without their skins.
- Drinking plenty of fluids to prevent dehydration is vital – If diahorrea is severe, rehydration solutions can be useful.
- Anti-diahorrea medications prescribed by a doctor can help.
- Try to chew food well.
- Try to eat slowly.
- Try to relax after eating.
- Avoid spicy foods.

- Avoid fatty foods.
- Avoid foods that are very hot or very cold.
- Avoid tea, coffee and alcohol.
- A course of probiotics may help to restore levels of healthy bacteria in the gut which can be stripped out by diahorrea.

Sample menu using techniques to help with diahorrea:

Breakfast	2 slices of white bread with low fat spread and jam
	A glass of cranberry juice
	A probiotic drink
Mid morning	A large glass of sugar- free squash
	2 bread sticks with low fat soft cheese
Lunch	A lean ham sandwich on white bread with a low fat yoghurt and a peeled apple
	A cup of green tea
Mid afternoon	A large glass of water

Dinner	Mash potato made without the skins with a cod fillet and a simple side salad
	Sugar-free jelly and iced low-fat yoghurt
	A large glass of water
Evening drink	A cup of green tea

Techniques to help with constipation:

- A sufficient fluid intake is vital, keep drinks to hand and sip over the day.
- Choosing high fibre foods can help ease constipation. Try high fibre foods such as fruit, vegetables, lentils, beans and wholegrains. However, adding bran to food is not advisable as it can interfere with the absorption of other nutrients in the body. Always increase fluid intake when fibre intake is increased.
- Gentle daily exercise can help.
- Bulking agents prescribed by a doctor can help.

See overleaf for sample menu

Sample menu using techniques to help with constipation:

Breakfast	Gentle stretching exercises
	Baked beans on 2 slices of wholemeal toast with a cup of teas
Mid morning	A large glass of sugar-free squash and an apple
Lunch	A ham salad sandwich on wholemeal bread with packet of dried fruit and a banana and a glass of milk
Mid afternoon	A large glass of water and a pear
Dinner	A gentle walk before dinner is served
	Salmon and a jacket potato with roasted mixed vegetables
	A fruit salad served with a yoghurt sprinkled with bran flakes
	A large glass of water
Evening drink	A large glass of sugar free squash

Techniques to help with a painful mouth:

- Try to avoid very hot food.
- Cold foods may better tolerated than hot foods.
- Try to limit spicy or salty foods as these can irritate a painful mouth.
- Choosing soft foods can make it easier to eat – choose soft versions of food or add sauces or gravy to make foods moist.
- To tone down acidic foods/drinks try adding sugar.
- Try drinking through a straw.
- Try taking painkillers an hour or so before eating.

Sample menu using techniques to help with a painful mouth:

Breakfast	A bowl of cooled porridge with soft non-acidic fruit like a banana cut-up
	A cup of iced tea through a straw
Mid morning	A glass of sugar free squash through a straw and a Fromais Frais
Lunch	A cheese and ham omelet
	A small pot of custard
	A glass of water through a straw

Mid afternoon	A glass of milk through a straw
Dinner	Soft spaghetti with lots of bolognaise sauce and grated cheese
	Strawberry mousse with cream
	A glass of water through a straw
Evening drink	A cooled milky malted drink through a straw

Techniques to help with a dry mouth:

- Try sipping fluids throughout the day.
- Try artificial saliva preparations.
- Vanilla essence can help to increase saliva production.
- Sharp tasting fruits such as grapefruit, pineapple, watermelon, peaches can help to increase saliva production.
- Try to limit eating very dry foods.
- Sucking on crushed ice or ice lollies can help.
- Suck boiled sweets or chew sugar-free gum, to help to increase saliva production.

See facing page for sample menu

Sample menu using techniques to help with a dry mouth:

Breakfast	A pot of yoghurt with sharp fruit like pineapple chunks or grapefruit cut up, sprinkled with a cereal of choice
	A glass of warmed vanilla essence and milk
Mid morning	A glass of sugar free squash and 2 slices of watermelon
	A few sugar free boiled sweets
Lunch	A glass of water
	Scrambled eggs on a soft buttered muffin
	A pot of rice pudding with strawberries and blueberries
Mid afternoon	Celery dipped in soft cheese and hummus
Dinner	Roast sweet potatoes, salmon and soft vegetables with a creamy sauce
	A bowl of ice cream and stewed fruit

Techniques to help with tiredness:

- Try out internet shopping – shopping can often be ordered and delivered free of charge.
- Ask a friend to help to put away shopping after a trip or a delivery.
- Make the most of the not so tired times, by doing the shopping, or preparing meals and freezing them.
- Make the most of the array of convenience foods on the markets, such as tinned, frozen, microwave and boil-in-the-bag. Stock up on these types of meals.
- Takeaways delivered to your door can sometimes be useful.
- Ordering meals on wheels for a certain time period could be a useful option, for example over a period of cancer treatment.

Store cupboard essentials

It may be easier to eat nutritious meals, if there are nutritious, quick and easy to prepare foods in the cupboards. Try stocking up on some of the ideas below.

- Tinned beans, spaghetti, ravioli, macaroni cheese.
- Tinned fish such as tuna, salmon, mackerel. Tinned fish in sauces may make preparing a meal even easier
- Tinned soups.
- Tinned fruit.
- Frozen ready meals.

- Boil in the bag fish.
- Powdered mash potatoes.
- Tinned, frozen and dried fruits.
- Tinned, frozen and microwavable vegetables.
- Tinned puddings.
- Packet instant desserts.
- Long life or powdered milk.
- Crackers that are wrapped in small packs of 2–3.
- Single serving packs of breakfast cereals.
- Single servings of cheese.
- Freshly prepared dishes like lasagna or chilli frozen in individual portions.

Techniques to help with nausea:

- Try to eat 'little and often' having small meals and snacks – Instead of 3 meals a day, try to eat every 2–3 hours or have 6 small meals a day.
- Try to eat sitting down and sit in an upright position. Try not to lie down shortly after eating.
- Try to eat slowly.
- Try to avoid foods that have a strong smell.
- Cold foods may be better tolerated than hot foods.
- Plain, dry foods may be tolerated well.
- Try to avoid drinking half an hour before and during a meal.
- Try to avoid foods that are spicy.
- Try to avoid foods that are fatty.
- Try foods that are salty as they may help ease nausea.

- Try foods that contain ginger as they may help ease nausea, for example ginger biscuits, ginger beer, ginger ale and ginger tea.
- Getting some fresh air before eating may help.
- Eating food in a well-aired room can help to ease nausea.
- Anti-sickness medications can help – make sure they are taken as directed, as taking a regular dose if directed, even when not feeling nauseous, may help to improve effectiveness.
- Try to sips fluids throughout the day, as large volumes of fluid may increase nausea.

Sample menu using techniques to help with nausea:

Breakfast	A small cup of ginger tea
	2 small plain biscuits
Mid morning	A small glass of fruit juice
	A small pot of plain fat free yoghurt
Lunch	A bowl of soup and a slice of soft bread dipped in.
Mid afternoon	A small glass of a fizzy pop
	2 breadsticks dipped low fat soft cheese

Dinner	A gentle walk before dinner is served
	Chilled pasta with tomatoes and olives
Evening snack	A small glass of sugar free squash
	2 ginger biscuits

Techniques for helping someone with food:

- It can be easy to make assumptions about the food and drink preferences of others, so it is really important to discuss and understand a person's personal preferences.
- Look at ways to help the person be as independent as possible, facilitate this by ensuring tasks are easy for them to complete within their abilities, for example setting the table or organising drinks to accompany a meal that has been made.
- Make sure that extras, such as sauces, seasoning and drinks are available – as these are important for flavour and enjoyment of eating.
- Help to make eating and drinking as enjoyable as possible by adapting to specific needs. For example, if suitable make mealtimes sociable and fun with the family around the table, without focusing on or talking about how much is being eaten. Get others involved with a pre-meal stroll to get some fresh air, or arrange

for a meal to be served on a tray during a favourite television programme.

Techniques to help with eating in hospital

A common issue associated with any kind of cancer treatment can be the availability and preference of food in hospital.

Being a patient in hospital and fitting in with set meal times can be difficult. People may be asleep or resting during mealtimes, or may be undergoing tests, or feeling unwell. Due to food hygiene regulations, meals cannot be reheated and some hospitals may only be able to provide snacks or cold foods if a hot meal is missed.

Treatment centres should have strategies in place, so if meals are missed or people are hungry, there is always food available. It can be useful to check with the centre what systems are in place and if necessary arrange and plan to take in snacks and food that are enjoyed. Check with the centre what policies are in place for bringing in food and make sure the centre is aware of any specific dietary needs or preferences.

Treatment centres work to provide nutritious and enjoyable meals and snacks. However, everyone has different tastes and preferences, and it can be very difficult to please everyone, particularly when appetite and dietary intake is affected. Whilst undergoing treatment, it can be difficult for people to actually eat due to tiredness, feelings of illness or being attached to drips and monitors. If this is the case, it may be useful have a little help from nurses. Having family or friends present at mealtimes can also be a great help, to choose suitable options from the menu or trolley and to offer a little help with eating and drinking if needed.

Tips for eating well in hospital:

- ✓ Try to keep nutritious and tasty snacks by the bedside. Fruit is often a popular choice, but it doesn't contain much nutrition. Try and go for items such as biscuits, nuts or snack bars.
- ✓ If well enough, plan to visit the local cafe or restaurant to have a meal of choice.
- ✓ Family or friends could to bring in food from home, such as hot soup in a flask, a favourite sandwich or a special dessert.
- ✓ Family or friends could bring in a take-away.
- ✓ If it is possible, ask staff to put a name tag on food to be stored in the fridge, such as favourite yoghurts, milkshakes or refreshing drinks.
- ✓ Some treatment centres may be able to provide small fridges next to beds, to store personal food supplies and keep food and drinks chilled.
- ✓ Family and friends could bring in a cool box or bag to keep foods cool for a while, for example refreshing drinks or fruit.
- ✓ Discussing needs and preferences with the member of staff who serves the food can be helpful. Staff may keep a record of these for their own reference.

✓ Discuss needs and preferences with a registered dietitian, as they may be able to arrange for particular foods, meals or snacks to be provided.

✓ Family and friends could ensure water jugs are refreshed and filled during visits.

✓ Having a favourite squash to mix with water could help encourage fluid intake.

✓ Keeping only a small supply of snacks and treats by the bedside, but refreshing them regularly can help to avoid boredom and food becoming stale.

✓ Eating by the bedside may not be ideal, so find out if there are allocated eating areas away from bed areas.

✓ Ensure that there is sufficient equipment to be able to eat, for example, is there a table that can reach an appropriate height and is there sufficient seating?

✓ Request to see a menu. Some hospitals do not necessarily display their menus, but they should always be available on request. Seeing the menu can help to aid choice.

✓ If the smell of food affects symptoms, requesting to move beds away from food preparation areas and close to a window may help.

✓ If the catering in hospital is not up to standard – make sure the appropriate staff are informed about the reason for dissatisfaction and any suggestions for how things may be improved. This can help improve services for the future.

Readers Notes on Chapter Eight: Problems affecting Nutritional Intake.

Chapter Nine

Fortifying the Nutritional Content of the Diet

Cancer increases nutritional requirements and can reduce nutritional intake. During this time, food may need to be fortified with additional nutrients.

Although a healthy, well balanced diet is important for good health, preventing weight loss, maintaining weight or weight gain, are often crucial goals of nutritional therapy. It is important to adapt the diet to achieve these goals, even if it means eating foods that are high in fat or sugar.

Preventing or treating under-nutrition will have more beneficial effects than any negative effects from eating high fat and sugary foods. However, it is important that if sugary foods are eaten frequently that the teeth are cleaned regularly.

Food fortification can really make a difference to the overall nutritional content of the diet. For example simply switching from having semi-skimmed milk to whole milk will add 120 calories per pint. If this whole milk is then fortified with 4 tablespoons of milk powder, this will add an extra 125 calories and 13 grams of protein. The volume of milk is still only 1 pint, but the nutritional content has been boosted by 245 calories and 13 grams of protein (almost the same amount as having another pint of semi-skimmed milk).

> **Food fortification can be an easy way to add extra nutrition into everyday food, without increasing the volume, which is useful for those with problems eating or drinking.**

How to fortify the nutritional content of everyday foods:

- If boosting the nutritional content of everyday foods is needed, then choosing full fat, high calorie options will make a good start.
- Increase the use of full fat dairy products like milk, cream, cheese and butter.
- Increase the use of sugary foods.
- Grate cheese into dishes such as soup, mashed potato or omelettes.
- Add bean, lentils or noodles into soups.
- Add double cream into soup, mashed potato and sauces or desserts.
- Add full fat milk into dishes such as mash potato or custard.
- Add evaporated milk to milk based desserts.
- Add butter onto vegetables, pasta and potatoes.
- Add syrup or honey to breakfast cereals or desserts.
- Add sugar to foods and drinks.

- Use plenty of butter in sandwiches or on toast
- Fortify milk – Add 4 tablespoons of milk powder to one pint of whole milk. Mix well. Store in the fridge and use within 24 hours.
- Keep high calorie snacks to hand – such as nuts, cheese and biscuits, biscuits, full fat yoghurts and fromage frais.
- Add ice cream to puddings or smoothies.
- Try to make fluids as nourishing as possible – choose milky drinks or smoothies to supply fluids and nutrition. Try liquidising fresh fruit with milk, yoghurt, ice cream, or fruit juices.

Readers Notes on Chapter Nine: Fortifying the Nutritional Content of the Diet.

Chapter Ten

Nutritional Supplements

There are many different types of nutritional supplements available. Some are available to purchase in supermarkets or local pharmacies and some are only available on prescription. It can be useful to be aware of the different types available.

Some supplements can be used within recipes to help increase their uses. There may be suggestions on the back of packets, or a website or a telephone number to call for further information where recipes and ideas can be requested often free of charge.

Over the counter nutritional supplements

Powders that can be made into drinks or soups and ready made drinks are available without a prescription. They can be high in calories and protein and are sometimes fortified with vitamins and minerals. These can be useful to boost the nutritional content of the diet by being used in-between meals, or they can be used to replace a meal or snack if it is not able to be eaten. It is advisable however; to consult with a health professional if these types of drinks are being used to replace meals, as supplements that are nutritionally complete would be more beneficial in this instance.

Nutritionally complete supplements

This type of supplement provides all the nutrition the body needs within a certain volume (i.e. energy, protein and vitamins and minerals). Nutritionally complete supplements are only available on prescription, so they can be safely prescribed and monitored.

There are many different types available and a number of different companies that produce them.

There are:

- Milkshake style drinks.
- Fruit juice style drinks.
- Yoghurt style drinks.
- Puddings.
- Soups.

These types of supplements should ideally be used in addition to eating and drinking. However, in some instances they may need to be used as a sole source of nutrition. Some people may dislike one brand, type or flavour but then really enjoy another.

It is really important to trial as many different flavours, types and brands as possible to find the ones that are most preferable. Some companies produce 'starter packs' that contain their whole range to trial.

Techniques to get the best out of nutritional supplements:

Fruit juice style drinks	Milkshake style drinks
Best served chilled	Best served chilled
Try mixing with lemonade, fresh fruit juice, fizzy water	Try mixing with some whole milk
Use in a recipes for jelly or fruit salad, trifles or fruit compote	Try adding to smoothies
Try freezing for a refreshing ice lolly or freeze as small ice cubes to suck on	Use in recipes to make rice pudding, custard, potato gratin, cakes or pancakes
Try adding to smoothies	Try adding to soups

Protein and energy supplements

Powdered supplements of protein or energy (energy in the form of sugar) are available, which can be added to everyday foods such as soups, without affecting texture or taste. In addition, there are liquid protein and energy supplements (energy in the form of fat) that can be added to everyday food or taken much like a medication. These types of supplements, often called 'modular' as they only provide one type of nutrient, are not as beneficial as nutritionally complete types, but can be useful for those who are struggling to have sufficient nutrient intakes or those that are unable to tolerate sufficient nutritionally complete supplements.

Readers Notes on Chapter Ten: Nutritional Supplements.

Chapter Eleven
Artificial Nutrition Support

Artificial nutrition support is very common and many patients in hospital and at home receive nutrition in this way. Artificial nutrition support can be given both enterally (via the normal digestive route) or parenterally (intravenously).

It is useful to be aware of the different types of artificial nutrition support available. The use of this type of support may be considered at different stages of cancer treatment, but should always be considered and discussed when someone is unable to meet their nutritional requirements from their current dietary intake or is unable to swallow food and/or fluids safely.

The use of artificial nutrition support would be discussed together with a health professional or registered dietitian, who should provide all the information needed to make an informed decision. It may be useful to ask to see and touch an example of the tube which is being discussed or ask to meet another patient who has had or is having artificial nutrition support.

It can sometimes be quite a daunting prospect, to be fed nutrition via a tube, but it is very common and can help to maintain nutritional status and is a vital aspect of cancer treatment and recovery.

Enteral feeding

There are a number of different ways to feed enterally, these are:

- Nasogastric feeding: Through a small tube passed through the nose ('naso') and into the stomach ('gastric').
- Nasoduodenal or Nasojejunal feeding: Through a small tube passed through the nose ('naso'), going past the stomach and into the first parts of the intestines (duodenum or jejunum).
- Percutaneous endoscopic gastrostomy feeding (PEG) or Radiologically inserted gastrostomy feeding (RIG): Through a small tube that is placed directly into the stomach through the stomach wall.

Nasogastric feeding (NG tube)

The procedure to place the tube is very simple and is undertaken by trained health professionals. An X-ray may be needed to check the position of the tube. The NG tube allows nutrition to be fed directly into the stomach.

Percutaneous endoscopic gastrostomy feeding tube (PEG)

The procedure to place the tube involves an endoscopy. The PEG tube is taken into the stomach and a small opening is made on the outside of the stomach wall. The PEG tube allows nutrition to be fed directly into the stomach.

Radiologically inserted gastrostomy tube (RIG)

The tube is placed directly into the stomach not using an endoscopy but with the help of x-rays to guide the health professional. The RIG tube allows nutrition to be fed directly into the stomach.

Parenteral Nutrition (PN)

Parenteral feeding is when nutrition is fed through a drip directly into the bloodstream (intravenously). This type of feeding may be needed if the usual pathway for digestion is not suitable or a person is unable to tolerate any food or fluids via the enteral feeding routes, for example due to severe sickness.

A feeding line, called a central line, feeds nutrition into a major blood vessel in the chest. The line may start in an arm, or may go directly into the chest. The lines can be placed under a local anesthetic, but an operation is not needed.

The source of nutrition used in artificial nutrition support

The nutrition used in artificial nutrition support is in the form of liquid feeds. These are complex, pre-prepared liquids containing all the nutrients normally received from a healthy balanced diet. In parenteral feeding liquids, certain essential nutrients can be added and adapted to meet individual requirements.

Some people may have all their nutritional and fluid requirements provided by the liquid feed, whilst others might receive 'supplementary' feeding, to enhance their nutritional intake. A registered dietitian would devise a specific feeding programme to suit individual needs.

The feed can be administered via a feeding pump set to deliver an amount of feed volume over a certain time period. In enteral feeding, feed can also be administered via a syringe, delivering a set amount of volume by the individual themselves or another trained individual. The feeding regime i.e. how much volume and how the feed is administered can be discussed and agreed with a registered dietitian and can be adapted to suit needs.

Artificial nutrition support at home

In some cases, artificial nutrition support may be needed for longer than a person needs to be in hospital. However, this should not necessarily restrict their discharge, as artificial feeding can sometimes be undertaken at home.

People can be discharged home on all types of artificial nutrition support, if it is safe to do so. This means that sufficient training and support must be in place. It is often the case that nurses visit people in their own homes to support and assist with the feeding process. It may seem quite a daunting prospect at first, but with training and ongoing support, many people successfully feed at home and can adapt the process to suit their lifestyle.

Readers Notes on Chapter Eleven: Artificial Nutrition Support.

Useful Cancer Charities

Cancer Research UK @ www.cancerresearchuk.org
P.O. Box 123
Lincoln's Inn Fields
London WC2A 3PX
Tel: (Supporter Services) 020 7121 6699
Tel: (Switchboard) 020 7242 0200

Macmillan Cancer Support @ www.macmillan.org.uk
89 Albert Embankment
London SE1 7UQ
Tel: 020 7840 7840
Information line: 0808 808 2020

Tenovus @ www.tenovus.com
43 The Parade
Cardiff
CF24 3AB
Tel: 02920 482000
Free phone: 0808 808 1010

Cancer Backup @ www.cancerbackup.org.uk
3 Bath Place
Rivington Street
London
EC2A 3JR
United Kingdom
Tel: 020 7739 2280
Free phone: 0808 800 1234

Marie Curie Cancer Care@ www.mariecurie.org.uk
England
Marie Curie Cancer Care
89 Albert Embankment
London SE1 7TP
Tel: 020 7599 7777

Wales
Block C Mamhilad House
Mamhilad Park Estate
Pontypool
Torfaen NP4 0HZ
Tel: 01495 740827

Scotland
29 Albany Street
Edinburgh EH1 3QN
Tel: 0131 456 3700
Northern Ireland
60 Knock Road
Belfast BT5 6LQ
Tel: 028 9088 2060

World Cancer Research Fund @ www.wcrf-uk.org
19 Harley Street
London
W1G 9QJ
Tel.: 020 73434200

Add below details of any local support networks for reference:

Appendices

Nutritional Status Monitoring Forms

These forms have been designed to make documenting and tracking nutritional status as easy as possible. It may be useful to use these for personal monitoring and/or in consultations with a health professional.

Body Mass Index (BMI)

$$\text{BMI} = \frac{\text{Weight (kg)}}{\text{Height}^2 \text{ (m)}}$$

Goal BMI kg/m²: _____

Date	*BMI kg/m²*	*Goal BMI – Current BMI*	*Review date*

Date	BMI kg/m²	Goal BMI – current BMI	Review date

Percentage Weight Loss

% Weight Loss =

$$\frac{\text{Usual weight (kg) – Current Weight (kg)}}{\text{Usual Weight (kg)}} \times 100$$

Usual weight (kg): _____

Date weight loss began, i.e. last date of being @ usual weight:

_____

Date	Current weight	% Weight loss	Time period of weight loss	Review date

Date	Current weight	% Weight loss	Time period of weight loss	Review date

Measuring Nutritional status with a health professional

Use this table to add in measurements that are being monitored by a health professional.

Date				Review date

Date				*Review date*

To interpret some measurements of nutritional status, health professionals may use standard reference range charts. They will be able to interpret measurements and discuss what these mean for an individual.

Index

About the author

Zoe Hellman Bsc SRD is a State Registered Dietitian and has worked in the public and private sectors. She firmly believes in the importance of nutrition and the impact it can have on well-being and health. This is her first book and she brings her considerable experience to bear, in the hope that cancer sufferers, their family and friends may benefit.

For more information on this book, and other books in the emerald series, go to: www.emeraldpublishing.co.uk